GILA MONSTERS
HAVE A DEADLY BITE!

BY ELISE TOBLER

Enslow
PUBLISHING

Please visit our website, www.enslow.com. For a free color catalog of all our high-quality books, call toll free 1-800-398-2504 or fax 1-877-980-4454.

Library of Congress Cataloging-in-Publication Data

Names: Tobler, Elise, 1970– author.
Title: Gila monsters have a deadly bite! / Elise Tobler.
Description: New York : Enslow Publishing, [2021] | Series: Reptiles rock!
  | Includes index.
Identifiers: LCCN 2019050638 | ISBN 9781978518223 (library binding) | ISBN
  9781978518209 (paperback) | ISBN 9781978518216 (six pack) | ISBN 9781978518230
  (ebook)
Subjects: LCSH: Gila monster—Juvenile literature.
Classification: LCC QL666.L247 T63 2021 | DDC 597.95/952—dc23
LC record available at https://lccn.loc.gov/2019050638

Published in 2021 by
Enslow Publishing
101 West 23rd Street, Suite #240
New York, NY 10011

Designer: Laura Bowen
Editor: Elise Tobler

Photo credits: Cover, pp. 1 (gila monster) fivespots/Shutterstock.com; cover, p. 1–32 (leaves border) Marina Solva/Shutterstock.com; pp. 5, 19 Vaclav Sebek/Shutterstock.com; p. 7 (gila monster) kwiktor/iStock.com; p. 7 (map) kateukraine/Shutterstock.com; pp. 8, 29 Tim Flach/The Image Bank/Getty Images Plus/Getty Images; p. 9 Steven Kaufman/Photolibrary/Getty Images Plus/Getty Images; pp. 10–11 Eric Isselee/Shutterstock.com; p. 11 (top) Terry W. Ryder/Shutterstock.com; p. 12 Mark Newman/Lonely Planet Images/Getty Images Plus/ Getty Images; p. 13 Jukka Jantunen/Shutterstock.com; pp. 15, 17, 27 C. Allan Morgan/Photolibrary/Getty Images Plus/Getty Images; p. 16 Vladislav T. Jirousek/Shutterstock.com; p. 18 Windzepher/iStock.com; p. 20 Design Pics/Getty Images; p. 21 rkupbens/iStock.com; p. 23 reptiles4all/iStock.com; p. 25 Robert Pickett/Corbis NX/Getty Images Plus/Getty Images; p. 26 Jupiterimages/PHOTOS.com/ Getty Images Plus/Getty Images.

Portions of this work were originally authored by Kathleen Connors and published as *Gila Monsters*. All new material this edition authored by Elise Tobler.

Printed in the United States of America

Some of the images in this book illustrate individuals who are models. The depictions do not imply actual situations or events.

CPSIA compliance information: Batch #BS20ENS: For further information contact Enslow Publishing, New York, New York, at 1-800-398-2504.

Find us on

CONTENTS

Creature Feature. 4

Home Sweet Home 6

Brightly Colored and Bony 8

Old Lizards. 10

Don't Eat Me! 12

A Hole in the Ground 14

Egg-cited for Dinner. 16

Big Bites. 18

Slow and Chewy. 20

Spit Take 22

Wrestle Mania 24

Little Monsters. 26

Future Gila Monsters 28

Glossary. 30

For More Information. 31

Index. 32

Words in the glossary appear in **bold** type the first time they are used in the text.

CREATURE FEATURE

You might think Gila monsters are terrifying, but while they do have a **venomous** bite that can be very painful to humans, they aren't really monsters. Like many lizards, they would much rather be left alone in their **burrows** where they can **digest** their latest meal.

Gila monsters are the largest lizards in North America, with heavy, scaled bodies. They look unusual and are often feared, which is why they are called "monsters." Once you learn about them, you'll see they're nothing to fear. Gila monsters are a terrific part of the **reptile** world!

Gila monsters like warm, dry areas because they are ectothermic.

GET THE FACTS!

"Gila" is pronounced "HEE-luh." These lizards are named after the Gila River in Arizona, where they are plentiful.

HOME SWEET HOME

The **habitat** of Gila monsters is mostly in Arizona and the deserts of the southwestern United States. They can be found in parts of New Mexico, Utah, Nevada, California, and northwestern Mexico.

Gila monsters spend as much as 95 percent of their life underground. They dig burrows with their sharp claws or use burrows made by other animals. Gila monsters commonly live in areas where there are plenty of rocks to hide under. These lizards don't want to be caught in the hot desert sun.

GILA MONSTERS' RANGE

NV

CA

UT

CO

AZ

UNITED STATES

NM

PACIFIC OCEAN

Sonoran Desert

MEXICO

TX

Gila monsters live in the Sonoran Desert.

GET THE FACTS!

Gila monsters may be more active at night after they've spent their day dozing in an underground burrow digesting their latest meal. They do like to bask in the sun, but once they've warmed up, back underground they go!

BRIGHTLY COLORED AND BONY

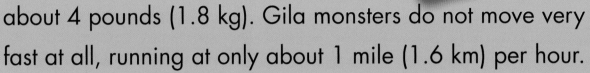

Gila monsters have short, fat bodies. They can grow to be about 20 inches (50 cm) long and weigh about 4 pounds (1.8 kg). Gila monsters do not move very fast at all, running at only about 1 mile (1.6 km) per hour.

Their bodies are covered with beaded scales called osteoderms (AH-stee-oh-derms). These are arranged in colorful patterns, often yellow or orange, and banded with black. Bright colors warn predators to stay away and not to attack or eat them. Gila monsters can live 20 to 30 years.

The Gila monster's skin is made up of small, bony scales.

GET THE FACTS!

Osteoderms are common among reptiles. Armadillos and alligators have them, and so did dinosaurs! This kind of scale contains bony matter and helps protect the animal.

OLD LIZARDS

Gila monsters have one living relative lizard, the Mexican beaded lizard. Gila monsters can also trace their family back to the time of dinosaurs. Beaded lizards that lived in the Cretaceous period (145 million years ago) may be related to the Gila monsters we know today.

GET THE FACTS!

There are only two kinds of Gila monster: the reticulated Gila monster and the banded Gila monster. Gila monsters are in a scientific group called *Heloderma*, which comes from Greek words meaning "studded skin."

back leg

tail

foot

Fragments of Gila monster scales have been found in **fossils** dating back 8,000 to 10,000 years ago near Las Vegas, Nevada. Sometimes, Gila monsters are called "living fossils" because their kind of lizard has been around so very long.

BANDED GILA MONSTER

RETICULATED GILA MONSTER

scaly skin

front leg

eye

nostril

tongue

claws

mouth

11

DON'T EAT ME!

falcon

Humans and coyotes are the main predators a Gila monster has to worry about. Humans usually kill Gila monsters in **self-defense**, while coyotes try to eat the lizards. The scales on a Gila monster are hard and bony, and make it hard for coyotes to bite.

Sometimes, eagles and falcons will also attack Gila monsters. Foxes and mountain lions have also tried to eat Gila monsters. The brightly colored scales on Gila monsters should tell animals to stay away. In nature, brightly colored animals are often venomous.

Coyotes will hunt Gila monsters and also eat their eggs if they find a burrow.

GET THE FACTS!

The Gila monster is the only venomous lizard that is native to the United States. It's one of two known venomous lizards in North America.

A HOLE IN THE GROUND

Since Gila monsters spend most of their life underground, you may never see one. They come outside to warm up and hunt, and then they crawl back underground. This keeps them safe from overheating and from predators.

Gila monsters are most active in spring and early summer. Later in the summer, they often come out of their burrows. This happens mostly at night when the sun isn't out. Gila monsters have been seen in rain puddles after thunderstorms, though they tend to stay away from flat ground when possible. They like to stay among rocks.

Seeing a Gila monster in the wild is unlikely!

GET THE FACTS!

Like many animals in desert environments, Gila monsters live underground because it's cooler and safer to do so.

EGG-CITED FOR DINNER

Gila monsters are carnivores. This means they eat meat. Although they are slow, Gila monsters have sharp claws and are really good climbers. They often climb rocks, trees, or even cacti to reach bird nests. They will eat the eggs they find.

GET THE FACTS!

In zoos, Gila monsters are usually fed mice and hard-boiled eggs. In the wild, they will eat frogs, rodents, insects, other lizards, and worms.

Gila monsters don't chew their food. They swallow it whole! It can take months for them to properly digest a meal. So, Gila monsters eat only three or four times a year. Gila monsters store fat in their big tails, and this means they don't have to eat every day like humans do.

Gila monsters love eggs and will climb to find them.

BIG BITES

Gila monster skeleton

Some people once believed that the Gila monster's breath was poison and could knock a person out. They also thought a Gila monster bite was deadly. Gila monster bites are really painful to people, but they have never killed anyone.

There are two kinds of venomous lizards in North America, and the Gila monster is one of them. In order to use its venom, a Gila monster bites, using its strong jaws to hold on tight. As the Gila monster chews, the venom flows into the bite mixed with the lizard's spit.

Gila monster bites hurt, but they aren't deadly to people.

GET THE FACTS!

"Venomous" means the animal bites or stings poison into their target. "Poisonous" means animals that give off poison when they are eaten.

SLOW AND CHEWY

Gila monsters typically use their venom for self-defense and not to kill prey. When attacked, the Gila monster will bite down on an animal's leg and won't let go. They will chew on the leg, causing the venom sacs in their mouth to let their venom flow.

GET THE FACTS!

Humans can run up to 10 to 15 miles (16 to 24 km) per hour! A Gila monster would never catch someone that fast. Gila monsters usually walk high on their feet, with a lumbering gait. They're not speedy like geckos and other smaller lizards.

Don't worry! You will probably never see a Gila monster in the wild, let alone be bitten by one. Gila monsters move very slowly, and you can definitely run quicker than they do!

Zoos are a great place to safely see Gila monsters!

SPIT TAKE

Scientists have discovered that the saliva, or spit, of Gila monsters is special. Matter in the saliva helps people with an illness called type 2 diabetes. It has helped improve the lives of many sick people.

Scientists have also learned how to make the matter in the lab, so they don't have to keep Gila monsters from the wild. The drug, or medicine, they make is sometimes called "lizard spit." In 2005, the Food and Drug Administration approved it for use on people. Another matter in the lizard's spit may help people with memory loss.

GET THE FACTS!

Like many other reptiles, Gila monsters learn about the world around them through their tongue. Gila monsters have a forked tongue like snakes do. They flick their tongue into the air to taste it. They can learn about plants and other nearby animals this way.

Studying Gila monster saliva has helped doctors discover new medicines.

23

WRESTLE MANIA

A group of Gila monsters is called a "lounge," which makes sense because they do love to lay around in their burrows. In the spring, male Gila monsters fight each other for the chance to mate, or come together to make babies with females. The biggest and strongest males are considered the winners.

Female Gila monsters are usually shaped like a pear, while male Gila monsters are more like an oval. Male Gila monsters often have broader heads. The coloring of male and female Gila monsters is the same, so you have to use their shape to tell them apart.

Males will wrestle each other to find out who is stronger.

GET THE FACTS!

Gila monsters tend to live alone, unless it's time to mate. Mating happens in the summer, when food is plentiful.

25

LITTLE MONSTERS

Female Gila monsters lay eggs. The female will dig a hole and can lay up to 13 eggs at one time. The eggs are oval in shape and about 2.5 inches (6.3 cm) in size. The eggs aren't buried very deep so the warmth of the sun can help babies hatch, or come out of their egg.

After about four months, baby Gila monsters hatch and crawl out of their eggs. Unlike human babies, baby Gila monsters can take care of themselves right away. They may eat the remains of the egg they hatched from!

Gila monster babies are cute but should never be kept as pets!

GET THE FACTS!

When they are born, baby Gila monsters are about 6.3 inches (16 cm) long. Gila monsters take three to five years to grow into adults. Gila monsters can live for 20 to 30 years.

FUTURE GILA MONSTERS

The United States and Mexico don't allow people to hunt Gila monsters. Big parts of the Gila monster habitat are within state parks, and this helps keep the animal safe from the harm humans might do to them. People want to sell them as pets, but this isn't allowed either.

Gila monsters are considered to be "near threatened" when it comes to their population status. This means their numbers are decreasing, or going down. As more and more people build houses and roads in the American Southwest, more Gila monster land becomes **uninhabitable** for them.

Gila monsters are protected everywhere they live.

GET THE FACTS!

In 1952, the Gila monster was the first venomous animal in North America to be legally protected. You cannot kill, collect, or sell Gila monsters in Arizona.

GLOSSARY

burrow A hole made by an animal in which it lives or hides.

digest To change food into simpler forms that can be used by the body.

ectothermic Requiring an external source to regulate body temperature.

fossil A leaf, skeleton, or footprint that is from a plant or animal that lived in ancient times and that you can see in some rocks.

habitat The place or type of place where a plant or animal naturally or normally lives or grows.

reptile An animal covered with scales or plates that breathes air, has a backbone, and lays eggs, such as a turtle, snake, lizard, or crocodile.

self-defense The act of defending one's self.

uninhabitable Not safe or suitable to be lived in.

venomous Able to produce a matter called venom that is harmful to other animals.

FOR MORE INFORMATION

Books

Hoena, Blake. *Everything Reptiles.* Washington, DC: National Geographic Children's Books, 2016.

Valdez, Patricia. *Joan Procter, Dragon Doctor.* New York, NY: Knopf Books for Young Readers, 2018.

Wilsdon, Christina. *Ultimate Reptileopedia: The Most Complete Reptile Reference Ever.* Washington, DC: National Geographic Children's Books, 2015.

Websites

Just Fun Facts

justfunfacts.com/interesting-facts-about-gila-monsters/
This site includes many great Gila monster photographs!

Live Science

www.livescience.com/58379-gila-monster-facts.html
This is a terrific site with in-depth Gila monster facts.

San Diego Zoo

animals.sandiegozoo.org/animals/gila-monster
The San Diego Zoo takes you on a tour of Gila monsters!

INDEX

babies, 24, 26, 27

banded Gila monster, 10

burrows, 4, 6, 7, 14, 24

color, 8, 12, 24

food, 16, 17, 25

fossils, 11

habitat/where they are found, 5, 6, 28

mating, 24, 25

Mexican beaded lizard, 10

osteoderms, 8, 9

predators, 8, 12, 14

reticulated Gila monster, 10

saliva/spit, 18, 22

size, 4, 8, 27

speed, 8, 20, 21

tongues, 23

venom/venomous, 4, 12, 13, 18, 19, 20, 29

weight, 8